BOA
EDITIONS
LIMITED

FOR THE KINGDOM

Poems by
Anthony Piccione

BOA Editions, Ltd.   Brockport, NY   1995

LC #: 95–75942
ISBN: 1–880238–22–5 cloth
ISBN: 1–880238–23–3 paper

First Edition
95 96 97 98 7 6 5 4 3 2 1

The publication of books by BOA Editions, Ltd.—
a not-for-profit corporation under section 501 (c) (3)
of the United States Internal Revenue Code—
is made possible with the assistance of grants from
the Literature Program of the New York State Council on the Arts
and the Literature Program of the National Endowment for the Arts,
as well as from the Lannan Foundation,
the Rochester Area Foundation, the County of Monroe, NY,
and contributions by individual supporters.

Cover Design: Daphne Poulin-Stofer
Art: "Genesee Scenery" (1846–1847) by Thomas Cole,
courtesy of the Memorial Art Gallery, Rochester, NY,
gift of Howard and Florence Merritt
Typesetting: R. Foerster, York Beach, ME
Manufacturing: McNaughton & Gunn, Lithographers
BOA Logo: Mirko

BOA Editions, Ltd.
A. Poulin, Jr., President
92 Park Avenue
Brockport, NY 14420

No one lives here in the mountains
but you can hear whispering sometimes
from deep in the woods, at sundown,
behind the faint blue light over moss.

—Wang Wei

CONTENTS

DREAMING THE FACE

Now That We Know Where We Are   /   11
Then Stillness, Then Longing   /   12
To a Woman Undressing at a Window in 1953   /   13
Dozing in the Drunk's Box   /   14
If Some Had Been Dreaming of Women   /   15
Standing Still   /   16
Discovering Her Face   /   17
Teaching, Lord, and the Last Shall Be First   /   18
James Wright Everywhere   /   19
Falling Asleep at a Faculty Meeting   /   20
Small Wind Prayer   /   21
Dreaming the Face   /   22

NIGHT WATCH

When My Wife Is Away, Time Fills the Cabin and Nothing
    Happens   /   25
The Night Skylab Was Falling   /   26
In the Gathering Cold at Christmas   /   27
The Holy Land on Television   /   28
Late Night Cable Viewing   /   29
Each a Word   /   30
Some Will Speak, Some Will Stare, Some Will Be Turned Back
    into Animals   /   31
Nightshift, Waiting for My Wife's Return   /   32
Calling Out to Sky's Mother   /   33
Another Morning   /   34
The Quiet Ones   /   35
Daybreak, and the Cabin Still Dark   /   36
Evening Bath   /   37

AIR

Air / 41
For My Students in Beijing / 46
Old Jericho Turnpike / 48

IN THE NEW WORLD

Now Is Our Century / 53
Walking with My Daughters / 54
Patching Little Things / 55
Medicine Priest / 56
After Napping by the Frogpond / 57
Poetry Reading: We Heard She Was Coming / 58
Now in the Birthsong of Sarah / 59
Surrounded by Everything, We Think to Surrender / 60
With My Wife in Deepening Storm / 61
Surrounded by Woods in Middle Age / 62
Poking Around in the New World / 63

HARD MOUNTAIN

Communion Prayer / 67
Ice Storm Heard from Bed / 68
At MacLeish's Grave / 69
It Was a Silence Settling on the Cabin / 70
From Far Off / 71
Cemeteries, with Two Sicilian Sayings / 72
Sabbatical Report / 73
Finding Hard Mountain / 74

Acknowledgments / 77
About the Author / 78

DREAMING THE FACE

NOW THAT WE KNOW WHERE WE ARE

It's time to start feeling our way again. We
    can call each thing its own sweet secret desire.

Since we were flicked out of the infinite speck
    just as we woke here from God wringing our hands,

it must be that the rocking urge or speed of stars
    holds our longing to squeeze into the dot up ahead.

It is good to lie down to die sometimes
    and good to rise crying inside a wild new face.

We'll need to forgive our craving for light, our mad
    passage from the kingdom lost, far back down the pulse

where the dark spark still hums forward as galaxies of fish
    and the shaggy heads of birds go on marvelling and forgetting.

Now that we know where we are, what took us?
    What the hell is this? What else have we done?

THEN STILLNESS, THEN LONGING

For he is five. He can sense and almost
see it split the northern star-dome darkness,
one tiny sand-grain meteorite of streaking light.
It would fit into a pore of the forehead.

He feels it shift, homing always to him as he shifts.
This takes a lifetime, fumbling along in dream,
the single glint trembling on through blackness,
and the body, even the body aches to rise and go.

TO A WOMAN UNDRESSING AT A WINDOW
IN 1953

A miracle! And if I was struck dumb by the chest's thump

I was a boy fainting in my grandfather's garden.
Face down, I wept, sinking through the body,
through the wet June stickiness too thick to breathe
in human breathing, in the root and stem-sweet air.

See these hands. We raised them to touch and to pray.

DOZING IN THE DRUNK'S BOX

Ask anyone, we were wine-hot pilgrims
set out to empty the pond by nightfall.
There was no home for us and, waking dumb
among the dead, we'd seen the dull sparks
flick from the wires in the President's vest.

We drank, spoke Cyrano, excelled in sports.
There, sometimes, in the ache and shove
you might glimpse, squinting sideways,
the calm five-point starfish man-shape
glowing at rest on the mud flat bottom.

If we sank at last to rasping sleep,
the waters also rose, and by dawn
the world was far, and darkly lifting.

IF SOME HAD BEEN DREAMING
OF WOMEN

At the last we ran outside, hands slightly numb,
eyes smoking, mouths open. A howling filled us.
Neighbors stumbled backwards trying to get away,
and now, over the world, what we touch falls dying.

Trees hurled themselves to earth all night,
waves flopped, slumping onto shore, exhausted,
and she, our soft, our only sign, has turned to stone.
Listen, you fool, where are you in all of this?

STANDING STILL

There was a jay rattling the air near the feeder,
one-eyed, tense, sending a call like an engine-spring,
all that he could say of his own blue-furred skin.
When he zigzagged out of here, everything stared.

Somehow death sings, half-sweetening when Christ is awake.
Some pray out, moan from jail, fight a crazy place.
Silence is listening. The stars sharpen their flares,
God's face packed whole in the last hot burst of time.

Now the sky was far and the heart gone mad of people,
every one of us, in witness for the One with no memory.
You can see for yourself the world going down at sunset,
a few watchers here and there, the lanterns spilling upon vastness.

DISCOVERING HER FACE

There, leaning against a rail, her mouth sweetly slack
and shaped by grief, by outliving grief and the small
twists of loving what will die, she is looking off

to the faint sea-sky line, out of time and nearly aware
that I am awake in her. The world tilts with it,
the sea lifts and lets go, the chest fills in a wave

about to deliver itself. I follow along, behind the desire
to sprawl dizzily in the saw-grass, ribs sore with longing,
the whole earth closer somehow, a soft, slowing forgiveness.

So this is our home where things ache to lie down in the dim
easy swoon. What we have done, her face endures. We are here
to weep, to touch the living shore, to leave our bones.

TEACHING, LORD, AND THE LAST SHALL BE FIRST

Exhausted, March yet stamps and gores my slow going,
and, dying in the drainpipe's thud and wait, my name.

Here, in the study, blue ankles chained to duty,
we will wake to their new poems. All right.

We'll measure a few more exiles, drink warm whiskey,
lie down soon in the sweet flat weeds without words.

But what is this, oh relentless one, oh soft and fierce,
oh burning laziness, oh yet and not yet? What is this?

JAMES WRIGHT EVERYWHERE

All day I read your poems out loud in the cabin,
half-sitting, half-standing, stalled in amazement.

Once, in summer, out at the farm, talking to poets,
we watched your eyes shift from praise to stare at the floor.

It could be you dreamed such loneliness was yours alone,
I don't know, but God bless you in your slowing hammock,

and God! since you left, everybody I turn to
looks a little like you, head down, in the light.

FALLING ASLEEP AT A FACULTY MEETING

You could age here for years without waking.
Applause around the table echoes soft and puffy.
I gave them my name once and sat near the window.

I must choose a new mind soon,
perhaps a cap and stiff canvas gloves,
wave from the red diminishing caboose.

Someone calls out for all abstentions.
No feeling in the hands yet, but I watch them
float, turning, and speak to no one.

SMALL WIND PRAYER

What's holy, then, sudden laughing
or the good sneeze? It all depends,
some say, on who disappears,
and who hangs back!

DREAMING THE FACE

Some rise up in powerful calm, in witness of being,
to point past the measure of self, that shaky science,
to strong feathery presences, of men, women, and perfect
first in the iridescent black face, the almond sweet squint
of moonlit Asia, the quick watery northerner, the spirit alive
of the softness inside, the world of flesh, the one you love.

There are those whose features barely mask
the stark machinery of body, nostrils twisting,
eyeholes stamped and sharply cut, steamy pipes, oily clips.
It stops us sometimes to glimpse emptiness facing us from
within, down a wet esophagus strangling in the light.

Most faces withdraw, at least when people are near,
not to a spite or tactic, but a secret closing over,
a watchfulness beneath the waters, as in the way turtles
suddenly are not there as you step on a stick.

It is not possible to find God, or enough, or even to grow old
without weeping for the exquisite distance in between,
but whatever it is we have done, there is a face for it.

Wherever we turn, what we can hold to and what we can love
took up our face when we woke just born and marked by loss.

We face each other, half-creatures, half powdery starlight.

NIGHT WATCH

WHEN MY WIFE IS AWAY, TIME FILLS THE CABIN AND NOTHING HAPPENS

The few crow calls echo more and more faintly,
already night has risen above the lamp post,
and I have stood gaping at the space
her car leapt into before it disappeared.

At home again, I love most what tenses alone
on spindly legs in the dark—twigs, thistles,
the long stemmed weeds, sensing the pheasant's
one-eyed stare as I turn at last and go inside.

THE NIGHT SKYLAB WAS FALLING

If I stand at the door
or hug myself in the cold
or rush out into the ache of evening,

I am near the one who waits no longer.
She gave up seeking the safety of things
and now the earth is at home in her.

No need to ponder luck taking aim
or why God lifts away when Isaiah dies,
so what use is fear, or planning ahead?

IN THE GATHERING COLD AT CHRISTMAS

Sparks fly up just over the thornbushes
into the faint blue glinting of starfires.
    Alone on such a night,
our lost brother about to be born,
waking first among the homeless, and the poor.

THE HOLY LAND ON TELEVISION

I barely move a fingertip, the streets of Jerusalem appear,
crowds part sullenly, an angry space keeps opening ahead,
I am only guessing, or the camera is what has weakened us,
but a voice says: *the work of soft witness is done,*
it is time for us to lie down to die, for just three days,
in the sweet muscular hands of our waking watchful Lord.

I don't think we can hold out here much longer.
What we have kept or given, or maybe decision itself,
has circled back upon us in a cold twist of heart, odd,
unblinking, and no one knows why, or what should be next.
The crowd tries to slow, but we are swept into the courtyard
by soldiers, though it is not their doing. They feel it too.

It is the air, something in the air needs us too much.
A minister comes on, a nice man with a maniac's smile.
Gray dinosaurs of love are grazing behind his eyes.

LATE NIGHT CABLE VIEWING

God, the astronomy woman is so soft,
talking about radio-flagging a billion stars
at once! *The first to shiver in radiant chatter
may be turning,* she smiles, *an eon from now
towards an odd sweet twittering light.*

In the yard a moment ago, my dog lifted
his night-measuring voice. A jittery leaf,
a creature perhaps, or the pelt-gathering
boy satanist from down the block, and so I am
already looking back over my shoulder, her face,
her words of stars swarming off over blackness.

EACH A WORD

Mostly they scatter when we call to them, seeds
too small to hold what they point to: love, birth,
awe. When we say them, light spilling from the tongue,
holy bursting sounds are named, and then the echoing.

We may forgive ourselves in this, crisp, efficient,
too late, too unlucky to change. There's no blame,
although our own scorn tightens on what we loved of home,
history, the unflinching faces in the photographs.

But night is our baptism of eye and thing, one pine, one kiss,
one blue feather, what kneels to be blessed this dark once,
fingernail, black light of face, breath of scalp sweat lifting,
of prayer, of longing, the sweet eyebrow arched to question.

SOME WILL SPEAK, SOME WILL STARE,
SOME WILL BE TURNED BACK
INTO ANIMALS

I click the t.v. on, my work done for today,
the room is suddenly too bright, a voice says
this is war, buddy. Short quick echoes
of shovel-gravel whacks make
the crowd turn its thousand heads.

Ted Bear, the champion, kicks at a chair,
grabs King Cobra Fahoud up, heaving
him through the breakaway window
of the small cardboard barber shop
out into the arena's center aisle.

Bear's young wife, Kitty, waves from the ring,
her smile a rueful wrinkle between two U.S.
dollar signs in clown glitter on her cheeks.

The fans are standing now, grandparents
and children mostly, drawn close in awe,
and they are laughing and wildly alert.

The snakeman must go down, that much is clear, although
it may not hold. This is too halfhearted, like neighbors
divided by a bit of bad luck. But a new chant is growing.

NIGHTSHIFT,
WAITING FOR MY WIFE'S RETURN

I have read all night at the kitchen table. Whenever
I look up, people are dying and being born over the earth.
Late moonlight pulls me to my feet in forgetfulness,
and because I love her, I go outside to stand with them,

the maples, the pines, and am received without fear or need.
Leaves keep scrabbling around the cabin woods and then silence
in the half dark. Overhead a tiny light, something,
shaves the enormous cold and is gone. My scalp knows it.

CALLING OUT TO SKY'S MOTHER

We go on falling
oh first one

past ourselves
dear grandmother

old *light and dark*
oh trillion trillion one

        head down you turned
        from all we had done
        passed once by the archway
        looked at me looked at me

the sky was closing behind us
the faces twisting in sleep

ANOTHER MORNING

And the body yet lives!
Glimpsed below sleep last night,
the infinite speck of emptiness
so vast it knows itself. My child
opens her door. Whisper
shakes the world.

THE QUIET ONES

Near sunrise, where light starts lifting from underneath
and things of our slow naming take their shapes once more,
I sit downstairs in the half dark, hunched at the table, still

dumb and clumsily askew in the presence of powerful beings.
The woodstack sprawl spells I! I! I! I! plainly enough.
My wife shifts softly overhead on her raft of sleep.

So I let them in at last, our two shepherd pups who
begin parading a kindling branch like a banner scroll
up and down the long plank floor, as then the cat from out

of the toaster box I've been saving anoints their heads
with an arched half-claw, first one, then the other,
for they, stunned, receive this so solemnly pleased,

and all the while the ivy's shadow gallops
in place above the steep split-log stairway.

DAYBREAK, AND THE CABIN STILL DARK

Night does burn off, the last folds of mist are lifting
now, and the long shins of pines reappear in their surround.

Calling to trees simply as trees, such stupendous belonging
moves me to stand at the window with my arms half open,

as I once did, in gawking witness, and my child
stepped glistening from her bath on wet wobbly legs.

EVENING BATH

1

I was filling the claw-toed tub we got from 1912.
The last of sundown slid from the glass-door wall
we put in when we lifted this chapel sized bathroom
out of the old slab woodshed. The plumber figured it
a joke, but we centered it, massive, facing south-southwest.
I was staring naked with a fine cigar into the twilight snow pines,
but I felt it powering behind me, my own bone-length sarcophagus.
So I stepped in, and settled to my neck.
So good to give up, and the body adrift.

2

When I rose in wet thick hairiness,
the one scowled back unblinking from the glass,
the new snow storming behind him, fist raised
to the curve of my death, if it went that way.
I've seen this man before, the demon gate-guardian
fiercely stiff, up on one leg in the lamasery door
I touched and took into myself far away once in China.
I, the keeper, collapsed, thrown from fear and hope
and called to broken witness in that unwavering place.

3

But I dozed, half remembering my oily promises to women,
I who smashed and chewed for effect a few wineglasses, wild,
fighting my way out of bars into the spawn lunge upstream,
who gnawed all night on the ankle bone of God, spitting blood,
the sirens all gone off crazy, streets lined with toothy priests,
doomed, wanting a home and willing to die for it,
but awake now in the face of grief, sweating from the bath,
and this, come for me naked, the body of my sorrow.

4

But it's our place to grow calm in. We built it the hard way.
So it must be that as I drifted, something powerful
suddenly weakened, cried out, and fell through my brain.
Either that, or they're calling us home again,
my neighbors, for this morning at the small village store
people seemed softer, unafraid. Some even asked about the tub,
spoke to me, they whose lives I wept for all my life.
That, or it is time to join the shaggy, upright creatures at last.

AIR

AIR

I don't know these fields but I keep running. The saw grass is wet, it is still mid-morning, and the air cups my face with hands upon a fever. It's 1945, I am about to be six. The wind feels good as I think this.

We've been playing out in the backyard, my cousins and I, maybe *Mother-May-I?* I see, suddenly afraid, through the white legs of trees, the massive doming slab of sky, unmoving, purely smooth where it rests just beyond the woods on the downslope curve. How easy, this secret—what is it what is it—and near all along.

So I keep on, waking to it and drifting, face in the wind of my running, arms out to embrace a roundness too big to hold. My chest is dizzily light, as before an incredible gift. It is close and it stays close, the distance across the field. I stumble, hurry, and always the sky-edge shimmers and reappears over the next easy hill. The earth is gentle, not a trick, this is what a sky does. If I will just touch it, with hands, the air upon my face a press of delicate skin. And I fall heaving, I knew I would, and cry, because I am happy, because I can reach, almost reaching, and feel through my chest the cool curve-turning coolness, the airy nearness in the air where the Lord moves, and I know it, once, and know I will keep it safe.

❋   ❋   ❋

It's First Grade and this is the first day. I have a desk in the middle of the second row from the windows, I feel happy, not scared, and these are my lifelong friends. Mrs. Lluellen is very very old. She has taught my mother and my grandmother, she says slowly and solemnly.

We are all sparkling neat, as for church. I have made a great discovery, and keep looking up the girls' dresses where they sit nearby, because incredibly I can see into them, because they have bright white panties. I look because I can see them and because looking is so delicious I feel my face burn, awe-choked, forgetting to breathe.

I can read and I can write out ANTHONY PICCIONE, my own real name I wept over when first I saw its tangled length. From some strange reasoning I know that for first grade you go to school one day, and the next year for second grade you go just two days, and so on.

All afternoon I play a game of holding my breath, the clock clicks on the wall near the flag, swooning past time to the deep sweet milky underpants of girls I love. That's all that happens. I love this day because it is sleepy and filled with presences. I do not know this thought. I only know that time is fumbling near forever and that it is real, of me, like this trembling in the chest when everything comes true, because there is softness between a girl's legs, because the world begins.

✳ ✳ ✳

We have to go. Our bus is gray-silver with blue, the lines of curve so complete when you stand and look your fill that your chest feels about to lift. It is 1946 and we are crossing Arizona in the desert. Greyhound. There's a streak of a creature on the side almost like a cartoon, but it is raised out of chrome and very shiny. The front paws reach all the way to the driver's window in long long speed. Seeing that makes it all feel solid, because there's a dog named for our bus.

We have come so far, my sister and I, with our mother. She is very young, but we don't know this. We just know she is beautiful, and funny, and we left Alabama, and we won't be going back. Back there is where the faces already start fading when you think them. We are going to California to Uncle Watson, our mother's brother. There is a picture of him, but his face is blurry and it's from the War. It is hot, all the windows open. Trees and poles whiz by once in a while but we seem to stand still.

My mother's face is extra bright. I say her name, Mama, drawing the vowels out until it sounds like I forgot what I started to say. She has been reading at her book, but she's too distracted. A few sailors, young boys really, are bunched around us talking, joking with us. It feels okay but a little strange. I'm wearing my brand new khaki uniform. It's starchy stiff, and I have Captain's bars, like my father who is gone to the War somewhere far and I can't remember his face, but he is a presence over us. The men are kidding me about the Army and how the Navy won the War.

One of them wants to know if I'm brave or not and then they all want to know. Three of them have picked me up and hold me straight like a battering ram. They pretend to think about tossing me through the back window. I am pretty sure they are playing a game with me, but it feels halfhearted. I even know somehow that they are trying to get my mother's attention.

The tires make a flat twine sound steadily unending, the desert blunts by with bushes and telephone wires, not bare, not empty, and the sailors make a show of rocking me far out over the side, and back into the bus. Air is heavy, prickly, oddly not cool at all. It's like sweating under blankets at night when something calls you quietly and you do not move and cannot. And I know, by this calm in me, I'll be brave, and am afraid, not of them, or of falling, but of the close, soft, unmoving point of stillness surrounded by speed.

❋　❋　❋

The bus was filling with darkness like a bedroom, not just shadows but everywhere, the air itself changing into something heavier. Around us all was bright day. Lunch was eaten, cheese sandwiches so real in cold wax paper. A man in a white suit came on when we stopped and our mother counted out three quarters. They made a solid *chunk* sound in her hand. Now she's asleep. Her face is puffy looking, sweetly pretty.

My sister gives up with my halfhearted dawdle at paper dolls and at last grows quiet, accepting sleep. The bus settles from side to side and seems not to move on in its speed. A baby keeps waking. Grown-ups whisper and doze.

Jo's doll falls over and I take it up. It's an old Indian woman in a red dress. Her face is real, like real flesh, only old and brownish with fat wrinkles. She seems very tired. It's apple skin made a special way, I heard them say. I can't quite figure this. I put my tongue on it but it's not like cinnamon or even stale apple. It is just the dust smell inside an old book, the taste of that smell. I take a small bite near the hairline over the ear, and chew it awhile, thinking about the Indians, and their hands, and how a face can come from an apple. There is something far off about it in the empty air and the delicate trust of sleepers around me in the dark. With a longing that has never lifted from me, I eat her face, the apple, entirely, with slow care, and prop the doll against my sister's arm. I watch it a long time, the paper-wad skull, the bosomy red dress, until the afternoon starts to fail and fall away.

※　※　※

There was a story I read when I was eight or nine about a place in Tibet, not a town but a couple of huts at a high pass where several directions met, and the caravans would come through because it was the only way for a hundred miles. The wind never dies here, ever, night and day every day all year. Air, then, is something alive like a rock only quicker, I thought, and sat light-headed in the presence of a great surprise.

To me air was one of those doorways, a hinge between real stuff and invisible things. Actually I pictured it as opaque skin with no thickness; that was as far as I could see. But this was so obvious, an enormous discovery, that I was amazed it had been overlooked all this time. Wind was something fond you turned toward when it touched you. And thinking of Tibet took me so surely to myself—separateness dissolving in the mind—for how could there be a *there* when it is in me, *here?* I loved questions like this. Where would you be if your parents never met? What's on the other side of the universe? And so thinking about God called in space, body, time, distance, speed and longing, the *almost* of anything.

I kept returning to that mountain pass and I could see them, people in baggy brown coats slapping the dust out as they came inside. They *chose* to be in the wind, to live inside it, and no matter what happened there was Presence you put your face into, or turned from to walk away, or backwards to. It twittered and sang and squeezed sideways through the cracks where stones came together in a wall. It cried over food, lifted your hair, shook your clothes, pushed hard on your shoulders. When the traveller gave a few coins to sleep on your floor, it was because the wind was great. Every minute held out a choice: go or stay!

I was busy with it all summer, my aloneness grew calm with it, and taking it into myself was like remembering. I would go to Tibet. Wind was a home even if there was fear to it. I learned my face because there was wind upon its shape. I have slept in full surrender out on the forward decks of ships and beneath the sky of Inner Mongolia. As at a celebration, I have walked out into storms, afraid and rejoicing.

I married and held it close. Our three daughters grew wild, and wilder still when we slept, my wife and I, in daytime. Good sweet noise. For this, we kept a small fan at our heads, a humming huff over the land to our pillows. These days I cannot lie down, unless there is air rushing over me, and the children are lifting their song somewhere, and the Tibetan foreheads are kissed in air and forgiven.

FOR MY STUDENTS IN BEIJING

You need this, I say, and begin each class with a poem read to their shy astonishment. So, morning in Beijing starts with the good poetry laugh. Today it's Robert Bly. "The Hockey Poem" has a big voice, I need four or five bodies at once, and I start acting out the parts so the words can come true.

Our goalie, Mrazek the Griever, is sweeping the claws and shards of battle but the oily Centurions keep coming, they want him to die this time. And that young athlete left behind in the motel trying to cover the double bed with his body, he's safe today. The sad grandmother of the woods has moved closer, her yowls are wilder just now. Actually the fear is right outside, up against the windows. We know we feel it, and that is why we love this powerful man. To laugh is to be suddenly everywhere at once. Bly brings the house down.

Night is so cold in China where I am alone. For hope and for fun, Friendship Compound dimmed or asleep, I walk my little two-room suite, naked to my sandals, reading Walt Whitman songs out loud to the walls. After an hour or so, I go over to the table and shake the black wires of my People's secret microphone lamp all the way to the ear of the expert English student who must be grinning in disbelief. *Whoever you are   holding me now in hand farewell now   for I love this life   as I lay down my head.*

I am taken by that student who must doze off finally with earphones clamped onto silence, and by my far away children, my daughters who told me to sing the words whenever I grew angry. I sang. We sat at the table, shoving, spilling the milk, sending double-takes skyward. At the edge of our clowning was the icy ache of the rule maker, to make neat, to make orderly, a coldness of fatherly, motherly distancing. We joked to loudness and the cold withdrew.

Yes, I was holding your faces safe but Tiananmen keeps howling. At night the hand carts are wheeled through the crowds, students dying or dead but somehow waving from that wobbly ride straight into the cameras. Out of range, tanks are dragging cold teeth over the great cobble square. We felt the world cry and draw in its breath. It may be that the world recoiled, I don't know. But once again, and still, something oozing with age arrives craving the lives of children. Here now are the newly dead. We should not name this thing, we think. We say it resembles nothing ever born over the earth.

OLD JERICHO TURNPIKE

It came right through our little town in Long Island, one east to Montauk, one west to The City, both lanes far-off mysteries and we liked that, we knew we were the absolute middle in any direction. "Of nowhere," our cousins kept saying when they came for the summer two-week visit. It didn't feel that way, though. The Jericho was a presence, as though set down from the future, or left over from a great ancient past. It looked old, anyway, made solid, foot-thick concrete you could see, where the shoulder dipped. We knew it was from Depression days, WPA, and our stretch of it was a celebration named Roosevelt Highway. We called it that anyway. Still, when you walked close there was a power and your bones began to tingle when you stepped onto it and stood there watching the two or three cars pass.

Going to Brooklyn was about as fine as it got. You started early, Saturday morning, Jericho to Southern Parkway, joined the sweep of light traffic, and the space between houses would start getting tighter and tighter. When they were all almost touching each other, you knew you were close. The '38 Chevy sedan, black, rounded by leaning into the same unaltering speed, was a place made comfortable by time and the blur of fading color. Every once in awhile the tires would scree over the steel grates of a draw-bridge. The stench of tidal flats, not unpleasant, stoppered your nostrils. Talking would go still and start up again. All the while the air grew closer, warmer, seeming about to change into something else entirely.

At last it was Bensonhurst, 79th Street and Flatbush Avenue. There were two cement lions facing the street from the stoop. Uncle Joe and Aunt Lena came out, then all the kids, cousins Larry, Pauly, Dominic, Angela, Tony, grinning and pleased. They took you in, you could say, with that hovering affection that makes you remember suddenly that you'll miss them always, even as you stand there getting ready on the kissing line. Uncle and Aunt seemed so happy, so enormously relieved somehow that we were there, that the world softened and made sense.

Uncle Joe was my grandmother's kid brother, so my grand-uncle. He was thin, dark, weather-hardened, and our great teller of jokes and tales. That's how we learned Sicilian, straining to follow the story, and even the yelling loudness was part of comedy, elaborate, the punch line set twelve steps in advance, and never was the rant-and-harangue taken for anger. This was the secret, our way of softening the Fates, governments, mortality, danger, the meanness of luck.

Grandma, mother to me, would finally get settled in the chair of honor, accept the single glass of wine, and her cheeks would immediately glow bright red. The hard years left her face so easily: this was her brother, and the jokes set her laughing to tears which she dabbed at with a handkerchief. I watched amazed. There was no sternness left, the Rock of the family swaying there like a schoolgirl so sweet to be near. Now the mandolin came out for songs. This meant the kids were free to go off into the yards and streets of that strange 1948 Brooklyn. My grandfather, the shoulders and the continent of our family, went oddly quiet, he with so much to tell at home. He sat next to Uncle Joe, playing the old mandolin, and watched his wife in secret, so pleased, satisfied, that she was happy.

In those days among the Brooklyn Rizzitano family, we were just the kids, but what was so clear was that they wanted us to be happy, to fit in, to stay. And they wanted us to eat. We did, into sweating stupor and delirium, beef, pork, chicken, lamb, lasagna and three other pastas, eggplant, mushrooms, zucchini, cheese plates, anti-pasto trays, tomato dishes, everything covered with tomato sauce and cheese, and the kids got to drink the homemade wine. Then coffee, then pastries, then a tiny glass of anisette. Aunt Lena, bright face sweating, sat back quietly then, more and more pleased, with that kind of radiance you see in the face of the long distance athlete whose task is done. She must have worked for days and now in the air in half-pantomime she half-guided, half-imitated the forks and spoons to our mouths. At the end, talk gone out of us, we sat around in the sweet pain of deliverance. There would be stick-ball in awhile, card games, more talk, cream soda, and sooner or later the long drive to Selden. But for now, this was it. This was all I ever wanted.

IN THE NEW WORLD

NOW IS OUR CENTURY

We know we've wandered far upon the human shore
for the leafy heart has left a crisscrossed path.

Because stars in the brain keep watch all night
and the earth goes on falling beneath our feet,

we send our only children on alone, and
the oceans are heaving with darkness and light.

WALKING WITH MY DAUGHTERS

Animals have left this path, they tell me calmly.
It is so still that we wait and stare.
Weeds stop lying down and getting up.

In the next field, three or four deer cough
and leap floating over the scrub oak. They are gone
as the creek sputters and everything speaks at once.

PATCHING LITTLE THINGS

I can fix everything at least once by midnight
and still help slab my neighbor's crumbly roof.

I may sprawl down a while in holy sloth
and join the creatures my father warned of.

What if I just lie here and hold out my bowl
where the world begins its moan and clatter?

Wait, I'll trade this place for a goatskin
and set off fast on stiff red stilts!

MEDICINE PRIEST

If I am a boy alive again and in my time,
then soon the priest will sweetly turn
to lift a sparkling wafer disk to the dove
beyond the edge of feathery paint and altar tent.
     the way light cups its weightless fingers
       the wings are trembling my chest knows it
We kneel as his hands pass over us,
out upon the four points of circle
up to the watchful star giver,
down to the earth one dreaming
and so to the guests the people.

A hundred neighbors start down towards the rail.
I am with them this once and ready at last.

     we go on mumbling in prayer, half-listening
      delicate bells begin to follow a small stream somewhere

The black doorways to the incense pot
The layering lift to slowness
The sweetgrass swoon of holy breath

AFTER NAPPING BY THE FROGPOND

Nothing to do. I pick the twigs
out of my shirt and open the wine.

When I woke, the sun was flaring out behind
a few swan-necked sunflowers in the stillness.

Now a rippling licks at the gnat-sized lights on the pond.
OH, THIS IS HOW, I say out loud, and cross my feet.

Night comes hunching in around me, right up to the mudbank,
I can see the scrub fields wavering inside its chest.

What's softening here, the spirit heart? Or something darker?
I lift my cup, turning it, as the peepers' song grows wildly clear.

POETRY READING:
WE HEARD SHE WAS COMING

She stares bristling like a pine grown full overnight.
Sparrows land, lift, land near her feet, there is something
about the place, we can rest here. People, when she turns

to them, throw down their twisty snares, one at a time.
But soon the air is flapping with poems, cornstalks, song of the
    apple,
of frogs, strong frog babies, feathery men, the wide winged-
    women,

out along the wild half-moon shore where she stands waiting.

NOW IN THE BIRTHSONG OF SARAH

Sometimes when you walk   dazed out through time
the hills and swoops of curves   behind those faint departures
the feet have just endured   there is the slow folding *oh*
you sense yourself rising to   dusk may be dawn
in the tongue sweet womb   aching touch to skyward
the wet breath is gifting   *oh* great patient heart thrum
here is a home   here on the rush of earth.

SURROUNDED BY EVERYTHING, WE THINK TO SURRENDER

—for my wife

Because we can hold each other all night
in the radiant dark in the only aching of things
that touches and forgets, we can disappear
and be received by the twelve directions at once!
In this we can love. In this we can die.

WITH MY WIFE IN DEEPENING STORM

We stop hauling love up through ourselves,
lightning keeps slamming the hillside dizzy,
the stillnesses pour back into silence.

The news teams may be out here by morning.
We'll be filmed fused in our messy twist,
their faces blank, but the good shove forming.

A few hairstems sprong stiff in electrical rows.
We go on lifting and joking in the nameless black.

SURROUNDED BY WOODS
IN MIDDLE AGE

That you, bird? My friends
have gone to live near cities
and my eyes are suddenly old.
Come down. Leaf, was it you?

POKING AROUND IN THE NEW WORLD

I'll kneel down in the driveway to pray for all breasts,
I don't know why...to shake the stiffness out of early spring.
The sky holds. Trees seem closer. The stars are risen.

A few lights are scattering beneath the ice and I follow them.
I try flapping my arms. Winds haul away at my raggedy blanket.
Night tightens a little around my shoulders as I fumble the joke.

Now entire villages are alive along the icesheet, a hundred small fires.
We may all be dancing naked, father, mother, neighbors joining in,
so that inside us is a wilder life, much faster, free of what we think.

But what's been whirling about, the mind or something farther off?
Cold has taken a home in my facebone, so, talking out loud, I turn
to the sky. We can live here I am saying, *we can live here.*

HARD MOUNTAIN

COMMUNION PRAYER

What we can hold to starts boiling as we reach for it,
the wet flat wafer aglow on the tongue, hot to warm
to ice-tip of touch, and then the remembering—taste,
aftertaste, the bright dot sinking to brainy blackness.

It may be we gazed too long on our own desires, or else
this is everyone's pain hollowing from below, silence
puffing like a pearly growth, the great wings circling
in the chest, the words wept for in the merciless dark.

Yet confession's left undone in the breastbone's tinny ache.
The watery pulse has pushed too far ahead. We say we can find
no trace across exile, nor shore beyond. We know it has left us,
this continent we flashed alive upon, and lost.

Let us be, the words go scudding, no better than all the animals,
majestic in passage, not knowing of knowing where to go, bowing
low to marvel in the leaves of darkness sparkling at our feet.
Deliver us, for this is the hour, for nothing we do can reach.

ICE STORM HEARD FROM BED

I fell and woke dreaming all night, alone
inside the slump and release of pinewoods,
each crashing to the weight of the earth.
At dawn I wept and was surprised to weep.

Across the blackness, I saw or sensed the faces
of our fathers, brightly startled, slow to go
but going in their light, risen again in witness
through the night, through the silvery dim centuries.

Power is down, the vines and veins
of power crisscrossing the fields,
and no neighbors, except the Amish farmers far off
who must be moving by now over the blinding slopes.

I think about them, and anything else that longs to wake.
Something unnamed, grief-sweetened, keeps calling us out.

AT MACLEISH'S GRAVE

I've been raking the oak leaves up to neatness.
A small plane keeps circling and finally breaks off.
I think my wife is walking over the next hill.

My awkwardness knows I am talking to myself
where he left just his bones and his name.
It's a brown boulder. You couldn't budge it.

I won't guess why we drove here. It's far.
It's warm for early May. Wind is resting in the grass.
I lie down stiffly to the all-way touch

of stars invisibly fierce in the daylight.
For this did we come out, marvelling and forgetting.
Faces go on half-forming, slow to vanish overhead.

The sky does part. Three crows riffle past
without sending down. I counted,
and now there are three silences.

IT WAS A SILENCE SETTLING
ON THE CABIN

A sideways rain, and the few maple buds go on leaping
through the silvery walls of twilight. *Things in time*
are close to thought, it seems, or maybe I prayed out loud.

Dog is safe and gladly home. I turn from the porch
to our cat stretched crazily in play, flicking
a brown-backed female thrush, flattened, fully alive

in that feathery claw-shaped kingdom. But this
is just our cat. I may start to them and stop,
pick a stone and let it drop. My head tilts, listening.

I can stand gawking, awe-sick, with little more to plan for,
let be daughters, wife, elbowy son, anything choosing to
move. This is love, isn't it, what we think, or do, or hope.

FROM FAR OFF

She is old, with a name like Miss Reese
or Reesing, a dry thin sound,
and she has waved us over to her old dog
the train hit, the droozy eyes still open.

This is Alabama. The road out of town
is red, deep clay dust, smooth,
with a couple of truck-track furrows
you follow to where it lifts onto highway.

My friend is black and gets the quarter.
We're scared, not of a dog frozen in dust
but of the ghost of the dog he points to
when I feel its breathing over my arm.
He stares, loops a long wire through the collar.

It takes the day, and he lets me stay,
giving rest, sliding it along again,
for the dead do not hurry, he tells me.
We bury it in leaves, praying and talking.
You can see where the wire still stings our hands.

I know we are young. The summer air is cold
where the wire has bitten, there is a red groove
through the dust, and this is secret work.
Now death is ice-thin and pulls at our hands
from far off. We stand witness and stop whispering.

CEMETERIES,
WITH TWO SICILIAN SAYINGS

It is your worst day, friend,
to be standing near a very old priest
who repeats your name with his eyes closed.

In July, grasshoppers overstuffed and wobbly-kneed,
I keep waiting for the grown-ups to remember me.
Time is packed down somehow into smell near tombs.

These graves are swollen shut but hot smelling,
warm to touch like big cake loaves. Arriving,
or glimpsed just now on marble columns, the few robed
witnesses fix the sky in their pale bulging eyeballs.

Up through the stalled viscous air around us,
the small blue jars and vases of watery stems
punch a dark green stench up both nostrils.

When a man opens his heart to the world,
we know we honor the boy sweetening within,
how coldly we sense his prayerful craving.

Yes, my sorrow is with that strange child at play,
but a leafy creature flew up and clutched my shirt.

SABBATICAL REPORT

Awake and up in the streaky dark, the way time calls me out, I can't tell if things of the world are separate or one or each inside the other. I start shivering, trees and scrubs go fading into fog, cold is a gray tightening, the great unmoving stillness is what the bedrock knows, not like bedrock, not the senses lunging, but the place itself. I have things to type. The cabin must be done by fall or else.

Five a.m. The good hand-tools almost gleam where they fell last night, heavy planks splay out into a mouth of teeth half-open in predawn dim, the coffee already cold and backed with light sawdust. My mail is lost or somewhere crimped in the mangle of bunkroom-bath we've been raising from the old woodshed lean-to cabin wall, and I underlined the memos for fun. In truth someone took the tinsmith shears to them and now there is a feathery tassel. Well. The floorboards are mostly straight. Running water's next. How strange words are becoming. A few poems, three chairs and a bed, our first hot bath, and it's only June.

FINDING HARD MOUNTAIN

1

The place was stiff-hearted before this, we're told, but
I start going dizzy just as the hammer turns against me
in mid-stroke and every third nail plangs out and follows
the shimmering lag-bolts into a time hole. When I fall
I feel the hills withhold themselves, the floorplanks heave,
shrinking into zigzags. Curse and prayer unravel together,
the dowser said. These mountains aren't from around here.

2

You still can't dig a post-hole without wondering about God.
That's how many rocks you hit. Or it's inside the rocks,
dragged down by the backs of their heads to sullen exile
where glaciers paused and turned away. Gray bone shards
and shore stones flint off the pickax into sunlight,
but the cold sparks of my labor will not lift me.
Nothing here will fit or bend or give in.

3

Nearly daybreak, the mountain is stirring, for I have prayed.
There is a home for me, then, even in new-world grief,
but when I touch the holy books, it is like the rain hurrying,
trying to reach. I think this clay rock knows me before I think.
Aching sore, far from grace, things yet seem playfully awake.
I still love the good joke, wild in the belly, so the tea spills,
both shoelaces break, my dogs keep forgetting their names.

ACKNOWLEDGMENTS

I am grateful to the editors of the following journals where some of the poems in this book first appeared:

American Poetry Review: "Nightshift, Waiting for My Wife's Return," "Poetry Reading: We Heard She Was Coming," "Patching Little Things," and "Standing Still";

Colorado Review: "It Was a Silence Settling on the Cabin," "When My Wife Is Away, Time Fills the Cabin and Nothing Happens," and "If Some Have Been Dreaming of Women";

Connecticut Review: "After Napping by the Frogpond," "With My Wife in Deepening Storm," and "At MacLeish's Grave";

Painted Bride Quarterly: "Now That We Know Where We Are."

"Ice Storm Heard from Bed" appeared in the 1992 Calendar of the Livingston County Arts Council.

"Teaching, Lord, And the Last Shall Be First" and "James Wright Everywhere" appeared in a chapbook, *Then It Was My Birthday,* copyright © 1982, Mammoth Press.

"Walking with My Daughters" first appeared as a broadside from Banjo Press, 1979.

Thanks to Jeff Lee for help with the Wang Wei translation.

Thank you, Rose Thornton.

ABOUT THE AUTHOR

Born in Sheffield, Alabama, and raised on Long Island, Anthony Piccione teaches English and creative writing at S.U.N.Y. College at Brockport. *Anchor Dragging,* his first book-length collection of poetry, was chosen by Archibald MacLeish for BOA's New Poets of America Series. In 1986, BOA published Piccione's second book, *Seeing It Was So.* His poems, interviews, essays, and reviews have appeared in dozens of journals, and his poems have been included in many anthologies. He and his wife, Ginny, live in Prattsburgh, New York.

BOA EDITIONS, LTD.
AMERICAN POETS CONTINUUM SERIES

Vol. 1   *The Führer Bunker: A Cycle of Poems in Progress*
W. D. Snodgrass

Vol. 2   *She*
M. L. Rosenthal

Vol. 3   *Living With Distance*
Ralph J. Mills, Jr.

Vol. 4   *Not Just Any Death*
Michael Waters

Vol. 5   *That Was Then: New and Selected Poems*
Isabella Gardner

Vol. 6   *Things That Happen Where There Aren't Any People*
William Stafford

Vol. 7   *The Bridge of Change: Poems 1974–1980*
John Logan

Vol. 8   *Signatures*
Joseph Stroud

Vol. 9   *People Live Here: Selected Poems 1949–1983*
Louis Simpson

Vol. 10   *Yin*
Carolyn Kizer

Vol. 11   *Duhamel: Ideas of Order in Little Canada*
Bill Tremblay

Vol. 12   *Seeing It Was So*
Anthony Piccione

Vol. 13   *Hyam Plutzik: The Collected Poems*

Vol. 14   *Good Woman: Poems and a Memoir 1969–1980*
Lucille Clifton

Vol. 15   *Next: New Poems*
Lucille Clifton

Vol. 16   *Roxa: Voices of the Culver Family*
William B. Patrick

Vol. 17   *John Logan: The Collected Poems*

Vol. 18   *Isabella Gardner: The Collected Poems*

Vol. 19   *The Sunken Lightship*
Peter Makuck

Vol. 20   *The City in Which I Love You*
Li-Young Lee

Vol. 21   *Quilting: Poems 1987–1990*
Lucille Clifton

Vol. 22   *John Logan: The Collected Fiction*

Vol. 23   *Shenandoah and Other Verse Plays*
Delmore Schwartz

Vol. 24   *Nobody Lives on Arthur Godfrey Boulevard*
Gerald Costanzo

Vol. 25   *The Book of Names: New and Selected Poems*
Barton Sutter

Vol. 26   *Each in His Season*
W. D. Snodgrass

Vol. 27   *Wordworks: Poems Selected and New*
Richard Kostelanetz

Vol. 28   *What We Carry*
Dorianne Laux

Vol. 29   *Red Suitcase*
Naomi Shihab Nye

Vol. 30   *Song*
Brigit Pegeen Kelly

Vol. 31   *The Fuehrer Bunker*
W. D. Snodgrass

Vol. 32   *For the Kingdom*
Anthony Piccione